THE BRITISH ACADEMY

The Rose of the Winds:
The origin and development of the Compass-Card

By

Silvanus P. Thompson, D.Sc., F.R.S.

*[Read at the International Historical Congress, April, 1913.
From the Proceedings of the British Academy, Vol. VI]*

London
Published for the British Academy
By Humphrey Milford, Oxford University Press
Amen Corner, E.C.

Price Four Shillings net

Windham Press is committed to bringing the lost cultural heritage of ages past into the 21st century through high-quality reproductions of original, classic printed works at affordable prices.

This book has been carefully crafted to utilize the original images of antique books rather than error-prone OCR text. This also preserves the work of the original typesetters of these classics, unknown craftsmen who laid out the text, often by hand, of each and every page you will read. Their subtle art involving judgment and interaction with the text is in many ways superior and more human than the mechanical methods utilized today, and gave each book a unique, hand-crafted feel in its text that connected the reader organically to the art of bindery and book-making.

We think these benefits are worth the occasional imperfection resulting from the age of these books at the time of scanning, and their vintage feel provides a connection to the past that goes beyond the mere words of the text.

As bibliophiles, we are always seeking perfection in our work, so please notify us of any errors in this book by emailing us at corrections@windhampress.com. Our team is motivated to correct errors quickly so future customers are better served. Our mission is to raise the bar of quality for reprinted works by a focus on detail and quality over mass production.

To peruse our catalog of carefully curated classic works, please visit our online store at www.windhampress.com.

THE ROSE OF THE WINDS:

THE ORIGIN AND DEVELOPMENT OF THE COMPASS-CARD

By SILVANUS P. THOMPSON, D.Sc., F.R.S.

Read at the International Historical Congress, April 5, 1913.

This inquiry embraces three chief points:—
 I. The origin of the Names of the Winds.
 II. The origin of the arrangement of the Rose of Thirty-two Points.
 III. The origin and significance of the distinctive marks used on Compass Cards.

PRELIMINARY.

ALTHOUGH the construction of the compass lies outside the scope of this inquiry, some preliminary considerations are necessary concerning the origin of the compass itself; and these must be stated briefly. The mariners' compass, as we know it to-day, consists of a light circular disk or card, beneath which is attached a magnetic needle or system of magnetic needles. The card is provided at its centre with a small cap, by which it is poised movably upon a pin. The whole is enclosed in a hollow box or bowl covered with a flat lid of glass; and the compass box or bowl is suspended within two hinged rings of brass to enable it to conserve its proper horizontal position in spite of any tilting movement to which it is subjected by the rolling or pitching of the ship on which it is carried.

The card is divided out into thirty-two 'points' or 'rhumbs' of equal angular breadth forming a rose or star, and to these are affixed the initials of the names of the thirty-two points. The magnet needle, or system of needles, is affixed to the card parallel to the direction marked NS on the card, so that when left to itself, the card, obeying the directive force which acts on the needle, sets itself in a direction pointing (magnetically) North and South; the several 'points' (or, strictly, *pointers*) marked on the card then indicating the several directions that the mariner may know in which way to steer in order to follow his desired course. The card is also usually marked at its North point with a fleur-de-lis or other distinctive sign. The magnetic needle is controlled in its pointing by the magnetism of the earth's globe.

It is no part of the present paper to enter upon the reasons for the irregularities which are found to exist in the directive force of the earth, and which produce those local 'variations' of the compass which the mariner encounters everywhere. Neither is there here any question considered as to the errors or perturbations due to the presence near the compass of pieces of iron on the ship, nor as to those due to the incidental presence of magnetism in the iron of the ship's hull or fittings; nor, again, as to the means for compensating those perturbations or correcting those errors.

The compass, as above described, has remained practically unchanged in all essential particulars for four centuries. The compasses carried by Columbus in his voyages of discovery in the West Indies certainly possessed every one of the features enumerated, save that it is doubtful whether all or any of their thirty-two points were marked with initials, and whether in them the North point bore a fleur-de-lis. As will be seen, probably only six of their points were so marked; and almost certainly there was no fleur-de-lis on any of them. For none of the compass-cards which have yet been identified as of earlier date than 1500 bear a fleur-de-lis; and those of them which bear initials carry only the initials of some of the eight principal winds. The windroses (*see* Fig. 7, Plate IV), on the Mappamundi drawn in 1500 by Juan de la Cosa, who was pilot for Columbus in 1493, have no fleur-de-lis and no initials.

Nothing is more perplexing to the student of the history of the compass than the unhistorical way in which the chroniclers have transcribed and transmitted erroneous statements and unfounded assertions, the truth of which should have been tested. Flagrant errors arising from bad copying, or worse etymology, have been sedulously propagated in the interests of mistaken patriotism; and the invention of the compass has been claimed for many different nations on the most absurd grounds. It may therefore be worth while to set down a few of the more important points as now established:

1. The attractive power of the lodestone was known to the ancients, as appears from the writings of Plato and of Euripides; and it was independently known to the Chinese.

2. The fact that this attractive power could be communicated to iron or steel by the lodestone was known to Lucretius and to the Chinese.

3. The directive action of the lodestone and of the piece of iron or steel which had been touched by the lodestone, causing it to point in the north and south direction, was unknown in Europe in classical times, but was known to the Chinese, who claimed for that knowledge

the date 1100 B.C., though Klaproth regards that date as mythical. The first authentic mention of the directive properties of the lodestone and of the needle is A.D. 121.

4. The application of the directive action of the magnet to travelling on land was known to the Chinese from A.D. 139.

5. The application of the directive action of the needle to navigation is of later date. It is doubtful whether the Chinese used the magnetic needle at sea before it was introduced by Western navigators in the sixteenth century. They had no pivoted compasses before A.D. 1297; and in 1680 were still using a floating compass. In Europe, the magnet was certainly used in navigation in the latter half of the twelfth century, as attested by Alexander Neckham (1157–1217), who describes the needle as mounted on a dart.

6. The first primitive form of mariners' compass was a floating apparatus, the needle being supported on a reed or a cross of reeds upon the surface of water in a basin. In this form it was used in the Levant and throughout the Mediterranean, as also in the Baltic. That it was in use in the twelfth and thirteenth centuries is attested by the ancient poem of Guyot de Provins (1190); by the maritime laws of Wisbuy; by the letter to Pope Honorius (1218), quoted by Bongars; by the narrative of Cardinal de Vitry (1219); by Baïlak of Kibdjak (1242); by Hugo de Bercy (1248); by Brunetto Latini (1260); and by a reference (1263) in *Las Siete Partidas* of Alfonso X. Roger Bacon in his *Opus Minus* (second half of the thirteenth century) states that sailors resort in cloudy weather to the 'stella maris'.

7. The earliest description of a pivoted magnetic needle placed in a box, with a glass lid, provided with a divided scale, and with 'sights' for taking bearings, is that of Pierre de Maricourt (Petrus Peregrinus), 1269.

8. In or about the year 1302 the improvement was made of affixing to the pivoted needle a light card whereon was painted the rose of the winds. Such evidence as exists points to this improvement having been made in Southern Italy, and in all probability at the port of Amalfi; but the attribution (by Mazzella in 1586—two hundred and eighty years after the event) of this step to a mythical personage called Flavio di Gioia is unhistorical, and the various stages in the growth of that myth can be traced.

9. Practically without exception, the compass-cards or windroses used in mariners' compasses were from the beginning divided out into 8, 16, and 32 equal divisions; the North point being distinguished by a dart, a triangle, a trident, a star, a group of stars, or, after 1500, by a fleur-de-lis. The east point was often marked with a cross. The

six other of the eight principal points were almost invariably marked with the initials of the Italian names of the winds. The rhumbs of the eight principal winds were usually painted black, occasionally blue or gold; sometimes they were painted alternately blue and red. In the windroses of thirty-two points the rhumbs of the eight principal winds were usually black; the rhumbs of the eight half-winds being usually painted green; while the rhumbs of the sixteen quarter-winds were commonly painted red.

10. The use of the initials of the Frankish names of the winds—N., NNE., NE., &c.—on compass-cards, seems to have arisen with Flemish navigators, but was early adopted by the Portuguese and Spanish. No examples of this use are, however, known prior to 1536.

11. The placing of the compass-card in a fixed position beneath the needle, as in miners' dials, surveying instruments, and opticians' compasses, appears to have originated with Stevinus of Bruges about the year 1595.

Origin of the Names of the Winds.

Long before the invention of the mariners' compass the ancients had adopted the arrangement of the names of the winds symmetrically around a circle representing the horizon; such an arrangement constituting a *Rosa ventorum*. The so-called 'points' of the compass are the names of the winds. Scholars have written much on the question of the number of winds recognized in antiquity, and on the names assigned to them, about which there has been considerable confusion. Apparently in primitive civilization the peoples reckoned but four winds, namely those that blew from the four quarters of the horizon—East, West, North, and South. Homer recognizes only four[1] by name: Βορέης, Εὖρος, Ζέφυρος, and Νότος. Four winds only are recognized in the Old Testament; see Jer. xlix. 36; Ezek. xxxvii. 9; Daniel viii. 8, and xi. 4. The same number is mentioned in the New Testament,[2] in Matt. xxiv. 31; Mark xiii. 7; and Rev. vii. 1.

---

[1] Σὺν δ' εὖρός τ' ἔπεσε, ζέφυρός τε, νότος τε δυσαής,
καὶ βορέης αἰθρηγενέτης μέγα κῦμα κυλίνδων.
                                                        Od. V, 295.

It is remarked by Aulus Gellius that Homer recognized no more than four; for in the description of the storm he says that *all* the winds conspired:—
πάσας δ' ἀέλλας παντοίων ἀνέμων.

[2] In the account of the voyage of St. Paul, in Acts xxvii. 12–14, four separate winds are mentioned. The passage may be thus translated:—' And because the haven was not commodious to winter in, the majority advised to depart thence,

Late Greek writers mention other winds having many different names. Homeric scholars have, however, found some difficulty when comparing these with the usage of Homer and Hesiod. For instance, Homer in the *Iliad* (ix. 4) says that Boreas and Zephuros blew from Thrace; and it appears doubtful whether his Boreas was directly opposite to his Notos, and whether his Euros was opposite to his Zephuros. The East and West points seem not to have been regarded as fixed in the same way as the North and South points. For the position of the sunrise varied with the season of the year, being some forty degrees northward of East at midsummer, and some forty degrees southward of East at midwinter; and similarly with the shifting position of sunset. Moreover, in different localities there were found prevalent winds which did not seem to blow from any one of the four cardinal points of the horizon; and these frequently received specific names, and were personified after the manner of Greek thought. For seeing that a cold East wind in spring and a mild East wind in autumn were looked upon as two different personages, one malevolent and the other beneficent, two different names would be allotted to them. The *Euraquilo* of Crete, and the *Skiron* of Athens are examples of the names of purely local winds.

Some of the local or topical names given to winds found wider usage, and spread into regions far from the locality of origin. An example is afforded by the mediaeval use in the Italian Mediterranean of the name *Greco* for the North-East wind which blew from Greece. But the same term became used for the North-East wind in Spain, where certainly it did not blow from Greece. In many cases there seems to have been no clear distinction between the name of the wind and the name of the geographical direction from which it blew. Some of the names are clearly directional; thus, the name *Septentrio*, though used for the North wind (in place of *Boreas*, *Arctos*, or *Thrakias*), obviously refers to the direction in which appeared the seven circumpolar stars; and the name *Meridies* (in place of *Notos* or *Auster*) is essentially the name of the direction of the midday sun. The names *Oriens* and *Occidens*, as well as the Italian *Levante* and *Ponente*, are obviously directional. But such names as *Euros*, *Auster*, *Zephuros*, *Aquilo*, and *Kaikias* are proper names denoting personified winds which seemed to have special properties, favourable

if by any means they might reach Phoinike, to lie up; it being a haven of Crete lying towards *Libs* and *Choros*. And when *Notos* blew softly, supposing they had gained their purpose, loosing thence they sailed by Crete. But not long after there arose against it a typhonic wind called *Euraquilo*.' In the Vulgate the names are given as *Africus*, *Corus*, *Auster*, and *Euraquilo*. The last-mentioned is a purely local name for a North-East wind.

or unfavourable. Attempts to identify the names of special winds, and the topical names of winds, with their appropriate geographical directions, have not always been successful; and the imperfect state of knowledge of geography prior to the fifteenth century added to the confusion. To fit such winds into an ordered system occupied many minds, and the developments were conflicting and even contradictory.

Probably the most consistent account of the views of antiquity is that given by Strabo. He was confronted with the fact that *Notos* and *Argestes* were used as names of winds blowing from the North; that *Euros* and *Apeliotes* were used for winds from the East, and *Zephuros* and *Dusaes* for winds from the West. Here he points out that ἀργέστης (whitish) is merely an epithet of Νότος; also that δυσαής (impetuous) is not a separate westerly wind, but is an attribute of Ζέφυρος, and does not imply or qualify the direction of the wind. That the wind which blows from the place of summer sunrise is called Εὖρος, while that from the place of winter sunrise is called Ἀπηλιώτης, he accepts, remarking: 'Exortus et occasus mobilia et varia sunt, meridies septentrionesque statu perpetuo stant et manent.' Of the four cardinal winds he regarded two as fixed and two as movable. We find other opinions in other writers, Hippocrates, Varro, Anaximander, and Theophrastus. Hippocrates adopted six as the number of the winds, but some confusion exists as to their directions. To the two fixed winds, North and South, there were now apparently added two sets of triplets, three winds from the East and three from the West, making eight winds in all, but they were not equally spaced out in their directions. The equally divided rose of eight winds is a later conception. But eight winds did not exhaust the number which had received definite names, and room had to be found for more in the disposition of them around the circle of the horizon. In Aristotle we find the arrangement of twelve in course of development. On the North, at the side of *Boreas*, he placed two winds, *Thrakias* and *Meses*, making a northern triplet. He also framed a southern triplet by placing two additional winds at the sides of *Notos*. At first these had no names, but afterwards he (or his Editors) named *Phoinikias* as being placed opposite to *Thrakias*, still leaving one (subsequently known as *Libonotos*) unnamed. The four triads so evolved are:—

Northern
- *Thrakias*
- *Aparktias*
- *Boreas*

Eastern
- *Kaikias*
- *Apeliotes*
- *Euros*

Southern
- [*Euronotos*] *Phoinikias*
- *Notos*
- [*Libonotos*]

Western
- *Libs*
- *Zephuros*
- *Argestes*

This arrangement of twelve unquestionably goes back to Aristotle, and is set forth in the writings of Alexander Aphrodisiensis and other of his immediate disciples.[1] It is, however, most frequently attributed to Timosthenes, the admiral of Ptolemy Philadelphus, who adopted it in his Portulan; and the arrangement of the circle of the winds, equally divided into twelve, is known as the Rose of Timosthenes. We find references to it in the writings of Varro, Suetonius, St. Isidor, Vincent of Beauvais, and others, down to the end of the Middle Ages, though with latinized forms of the names in Western Europe. In the meantime Eratosthenes had modified the scheme in two ways. Whereas the Aristotelians had viewed the winds as issuing from different points, Eratosthenes assigned to them definite spaces or regions, which, according to Vitruvius, were of equal width; and he had simplified the arrangement by fixing the number of spaces as eight.[2] To this system the fundamental witness is the Tower of the Winds at Athens, erected about 100 B.C. by Andronicus Cyrrhestes. It has eight flanks facing the eight winds, each adorned with an emblematic figure in relief, as follows: *Boreas, Kaikias, Apeliotes, Euros, Notos, Lips, Zephuros,* and *Skiron*. Pliny, in his *Natural History*, refers to the schemes of four and twelve winds, and adds that 'the Moderne sailers of late daies, founde out a meane betweene both: and they put unto that short number of the first, foure winds and no more, which they tooke out of the later. Therefore every quarter of the heaven hath two winds apeece." From the equinoctiall sunne-rising bloweth the East wind *Subsolanus*: from the rising thereof in Mid-winter, the Southeast *Vulturnus*. The former of these the Greekes call *Apeliotes*, and the later *Eurus*. From the mid-day riseth the South wind [*Auster*]: and from the sunne-setting in Midwinter the Southwest, *Africus*. They also name these two *Notus* and *Libs*. From the equinoctiall going downe of the Sunne, the West wind *Favonius* commeth, but from that in Summer season, the Northwest *Corus*; and by the same Greekes they are tearmed *Zephyrus* and *Argestes*. From the North-waine or pole Arctike, bloweth the North wind *Septentrio*: betweene which and the Sunne-rising in Summer, is the Northeast wind *Aquilo*, named *Aparctias* and *Boreas* by the Greekes.'[3]

[1] For a later example of the unequally-divided rose of twelve winds, four principal and eight collateral, see Schöner's *Opusculum Geographicum*, Nürnberg, 1533, which gives the names in Latin and Greek.

[2] Vitruvius also gives a diagram of twenty-four named winds; but this rose never found acceptance either on land or at sea.

[3] *The Historie of the World.* Philemon Holland's Translation (London, 1601), p. 22.

The rose of twelve winds continued to be used, and is found in Seneca and later writers, using the Latin names, down to the *Margarita Philosophica* of Reisch in the sixteenth century. The northern nations had never possessed, however, such a multiplicity of names. Eginhard,[1] in his life of Charles the Great, narrates how that monarch, at the beginning of the ninth century, finding in the Teutonic tongues the names of the four cardinal points only, combined them two-and-two in such a way as to denote the twelve winds, as follows :—

Circius	Nordwestren
Septentrio	Nordren
Aquilo	Nordostren
Vulturnus	Ostnorden
Subsolanus	Ostren
Eurus	Ostsundren
Euroauster	Sundostren
Auster	Sundren
Austroafricus	Sundwestren
Africus	Westsundren
Zephyrus	Westren
Chorus	Westnordren

This notation, with some slight changes, was repeated in the *Hortus Deliciarum* of the Abbess Herrade de Londsberg, in the eleventh century, in a magnificent Manuscript which unfortunately perished in the fire of the Library of Strassburg, in the siege of 1870. The same scheme appears again in the fourteenth century on a planisphere in a Latin Manuscript in the Library of Arras, but with further variations, the form of which suggests that by that time another Frankish adaptation to sixteen winds had already become current. The Paris edition, 1555, of Orontius Finaeus, *De Mundi Sphera sive Cosmographia*, gives two windroses of sixteen points with the Frankish names; and the author comments on the circumstance that the making-up of the names of the subsidiary points by combining the names of the four cardinal winds imposed the adoption of monosyllables for those four. The Flemish mariners, and particularly those of Bruges, early adopted these Frankish terms; and the tradition is recurrent that the actual denominations of the thirty-two points, as used throughout all Europe to-day, were framed by the pilots of Bruges.

The Latin rose of twelve winds had found acceptance throughout the Roman Empire from Egypt to Spain, and continued through

[1] Eginhard, *Vita et Gesta Karoli Magni*, p. 34.

the Middle Ages. It appears in the *De Natura Rerum* of St. Isidor, and in the work of the same name by the Venerable Bede. It occurs in the *Cosmographie* of Azaph, about the end of the eleventh century. It is repeated by Vincent de Beauvais and by Albertus Magnus. It reappears in the famous Mappamundi in the Cathedral Library of Hereford, in the *Polychronicon* of Higden (1357), and in the *De Proprietatibus Rerum* of his contemporary Bartholomeus de Glanvilla. Most of the fifteenth and sixteenth-century editions of the *Geographia* of Claudius Ptolemaeus give the rose of twelve winds. Nevertheless, a transition from the rose of twelve to the rose of eight winds, with its subdivisions into sixteen and thirty-two, by the interposition of half-winds and quarter-winds, was in progress. The same kind of simplification which Eratosthenes had effected in the system of Aristotle was to be repeated, but with the accompanying gain of a more minute secondary and tertiary subdivision. The transition was accompanied by a change too in the current names. The *Cosmographie* of Azaph, cited above for an example of the rose of twelve, exhibits this transition in process, for it gives also a planisphere with eight. In the somewhat later *Livres dou Tresor* of Ser Brunetto Latini the same simplification appears, and the names adopted by these two writers may be compared.

Azaph	Brunetto Latini
Tramontana	*Tramontainne*
Graecus	*Grec*
Oriens	*Levant*
Sillocus (or *Imber*)	*Siloc*
Meridies	*Midi*
Garbinus (or *Lebex*)	*Aufrique* (or *Garb*, or *Lebech*)
Occidens	*Couchant*
Magister	*Maistre*

Here we meet with the arrangement destined to supersede the classical twelve-point rose, namely, that which, because it better satisfied nautical needs, won its way amongst the seamen of the Mediterranean. They modified the names by substitution of vernacular equivalents, using *Levante* for *Oriens*, and *Ponente* for *Occidens*. For *Meridies* they adopted *Ostro*, the Italian form of the classical *Auster*, while for *Garbin* or *Lebex* (which appears to be of Arabic origin) they more commonly used *Africo*, though *Libeccio* (or *Labetes*, or even *Le Bex*) continued also as a synonym. In this list of the eight winds of Azaph we meet for the first time with two new names, that of *Magister* for the North West wind, and that of *Sillocus* for the South East wind. The occurrence of these two names fixes the origin of the system in the Italian Mediterranean, just as surely as does the occurrence of the other terms *Greco, Africo,* and *Tramontana.* In the Mappamundi of Marino Sanudo, of 1321 (now in Brussels), the eight names are given in Italian. A comment on the date of this transition from the twelve-point rose to the eight-point or sixteen-point rose is afforded by the circumstance that while in the poem (middle fifteenth century) entitled *La Sfera,* of Gregorio Dati, there are several stanzas in ottava rima recounting by name the twelve winds, we find in the kindred poem called *La Nuova Sfera,* of Joannes Maria Tolosani, published in 1514 at Florence, four stanzas similarly reciting the names and virtues of the sixteen winds. In Italy, and throughout Southern Europe, the name *Magister* for the favourable North West wind is preserved to us in the familiar form of *Maestro. Sillocus,* for the South East wind, is the familiar *Scirocco,* which reappears in subsequent windroses and charts under many forms: *Silocco,* or *Sirocco,* on the Pisan charts; *Siloc,* in Brunetto Latini; *Exaloch,* in the *Ars Magna* of Lully; *Laxaloch,* on the Catalan Atlas; *Issalot,* in the *Lexique Roman* of Raynouard; *Xaloque* and *Saluq* in certain Arabic sailing-charts.

Such then was the order of developments which issued in the eight-point windrose, with its Italian names. What the influence of the Crusades was in bringing about its adoption is a matter for conjecture only. It remains to be remarked that the Portuguese mariners at an early date seem to have adopted the Flemish designations of the winds in preference to the Italian. In the *Arte de navegar,* of Pedro de Medina (Valladolid, 1545), the Flemish names of the winds are given, and are displayed variously in roses of four, eight, twelve, and thirty-two points. Roderigo Camorana, in his *Compendio del Arte de navegar* (Seville, 1588), uses always the Flemish names. Flemish designations appear also in the windrose in the chart of Ruiz de Estrada e Peñato (1525). Flemish names are exclusively used in the *Trattado da Agulha de marear* written by João de Lisboa in 1514 (printed 1903 at Lisbon). The Jesuit writers of the seventeenth century—Kircher, De Lanis, Dechales, Riccioli, and Fournier—give elaborate tables of the names of the winds in various languages. Dechales (*Cursus Mathematicus,* 1674, T. ii, p. 250) points out at some length the differences in usage between Southern Europe and Northern. The drawings of compasses given by Nuñez (1536), Martinus Cortes (Seville, 1556) and Pedro de Medina (Valladolid, 1545) bear the names or initials of the Flemish winds, though the last-named also gives one with Italian initials. A rose of thirty-two points drawn by Willebrord Snell in his *Tiphys Batavus* (Lugd. Batav., 1624) gives the full names in Dutch: Noort, Noort-ten-oosten, Noort-noort-oost, Noort-oost-ten-noorden, Noort-oost, &c.

In the works of the contemporary cosmographers we meet with many diagrams of the winds, usually depicted around the planisphere or map by cherubs' heads blowing. The various editions of the *Cosmographia* of Pietro d' Abano (Bienewicz) are rich in such. The

Cecco d'Ascoli. 1521.

Antwerp edition of 1533, fol. 27, shows twelve cherubs' heads with names in three languages. The *Arte de navegar* of Pedro de Medina (1545) gives a planisphere surrounded by eight cherubs' heads. The *Cosmographia* of Barocio (Venice, 1585) gives one planisphere with four cherubs, another with twelve, another with thirty-two, large and small. A Mappamundi in the Cologne edition of Macrobius, of 1521, depicts sixteen cherubs, the four principal ones being within the periphery, and the twelve auxiliary ones grouped in triads outside.

The Milan edition of the *Acerba* of Cecco d' Ascoli (F. de Stabili), of the same date, contains a remarkable cut—the earliest known professed picture of a compass in any printed book—of the Italian eight-point rose, having the usual initials and cross marked upon its rays, and the names of the winds printed opposite each in the margin. Between the eight rays are eight cherubs' heads blowing. (*See* page 11.)

Origin of the Arrangement of the Rose of Thirty-two Points.

'It is certain that so soon as the compass was used for sailing, the division of the horizon into eight or twelve winds was found altogether insufficient for the purposes of navigation. On the other hand the division of each quadrant into ninety degrees, as proposed by Pierre de Maricourt (Petrus Peregrinus) in 1269, was too fine to be practical. Division into thirty-two by the intercalation, between the eight principal winds, of eight half-winds and sixteen quarter-winds, by successive bisection of the angles, afforded the most natural way of attaining the requisite precision.' Whatever the plan retained by geographers for the delineation of their land-maps, nautical chartographers from the thirteenth century onwards preferred the division into eight, sixteen, and thirty-two. As authorities for this statement may be cited Chaucer,[1] Schöner,[2] Nuñez,[3] and Riccioli.[4] The last-named says expressly that the division into thirty-two winds has been exclusively employed, since the time of Carolus Magnus, by chartographers and seamen. Prior to the introduction of the primitive compass, seamen in the Levant and in the western part of the Mediterranean could not direct their courses, when out of sight of land, with any precision. This circumstance undoubtedly accounts for two facts: (1) that their navigation was—at any rate in doubtful weather—largely confined to coasting routes; (2) that their primitive maps were exceedingly crude. With the introduction of the compass the sailing of direct courses became comparatively safe and habitual; and, with the knowledge of the direction in which their courses were set, they were able to delineate, with far greater precision than before, the outlines of the coasts in the sailing-charts which almost suddenly superseded the older forms of map. It is, indeed, impossible to sever the develop-

---

[1] Chaucer, *The Astrolabe*, Pt. 2, § 31, 1390.
[2] Schöner, *Opusculum Geographicum*, Norimb., 1533.
[3] Nuñez, MS. of sixteenth century in Bibl. Nat., Paris.
[4] Riccioli, *Almagestum novum*, Lib. II, cap. xvi, De Ventis, Bononiae, 1651.

ment of the compass from that of the sailing-chart. The more closely one regards the question, the more insistently is one convinced of the immense changes brought about by the introduction of the compass. In mere coasting, the important thing to know is the distance from port to port, and the aspects of the various headlands. Angular distances are of relatively little moment. But in sea-sailing the direction is everything, and distances are of secondary importance. The character of such charts and maps as have come down to us from pre-compass times may be judged by the typical examples of the maps accredited to Ptolemy, in which the directions of the coast lines are often ludicrously wrong, while the distances from port to port are carefully stated. The Portulani, or haven-finding guides, to direct the mariner from port to port, laborious compilations of distances and landmarks along the routes, were in abundant use before the advent of real sailing-charts, and go back to the Byzantine *Stadiasmos* of the fourth or fifth century, now in Madrid. A late example, in English, of this kind of treatise is *The Safeguard of Saylers, or Great Rutter*, of Robert Norman, printed in London in 1590.

Totally distinct from all the earlier maps, planispheres, mappae-mundi, and other primitive forms, are the *sailing-charts* which made their appearance at the outset of the fourteenth century. The most characteristic thing about them, distinguishing them from all previous kinds of map, is the presence of the so-called loxodromic lines, presenting a system of rays, starting usually from some central point, and uniting a subsidiary series of centres arranged in a circle around the map, which becomes covered as with a web of fine lines. These lines are supposed to indicate direct routes along the recognized directions of the winds; hence the term *loxodromic*. That they indicate straight courses can, naturally, only be true upon the assumption that the projection of the map is a true projection on a plane (as in the method of projection known as Mercator's), and in this case the distances are distorted, the scale at the margins being different from that at the centre. When, however, so small a part of the whole globe as the Mediterranean region is all that is represented, the scale of distances will not vary greatly between different parts of the same map, and the loxodromic lines will practically represent straight courses. The vast majority of the sailing-charts in question are of Italian origin, most of them executed by Italian chartographers; and they present a number of features in common which distinguish them from all other maps. They are all executed on parchment, and almost invariably on single skins. They all have the loxodromic lines. These lines are almost without exception thirty-two[1] in number, very rarely eight or sixteen. The lines are invariably drawn in colour: the eight principal winds black; the eight half-winds green (rarely blue); the sixteen quarter-winds red.[2] At the centre of the network of loxodromic lines, at least in the charts after 1375, there is usually depicted a decorative *rosa ventorum*, gaily coloured; and at one or more subsidiary points serving as centres for other systems of loxodromic lines other roses or rosettes are frequently painted. On comparing chart with chart it is seen that these loxodromic centres are differently chosen in different maps, there being no fixed point,[3] no meridian of Greenwich, nor of Rome, nor of Naples, not even of Jerusalem. Nor is there any fixed size of radius for the network of lines. Most of these charts depict the seaboard almost exclusively, and give the names of places on the coast, but rarely the names of inland places; nor do they give many inland features beyond vague indications of mountain ranges or forests. The later charts mark political divisions by heraldic banners or devices, or by figures of eastern potentates, and in some the cities are indicated by conventional castles or churches. Wild animals, camels, elephants, lions, bears, and reindeer adorn the outlying regions of the later maps.

---

[1] Santarem, vol. i, p. 275 of his *Essai sur l'histoire de la cosmographie et de la cartographie pendant le moyen âge*, erroneously states that there are no charts with thirty-two rhumbs upon them before the Pizigani chart of 1367; and he argues fallaciously that Italian and Catalan sailors had never undertaken navigation on the high seas before the Portuguese expeditions to the Canaries from 1331 to 1344. The sailing-charts of the priest Giovanni da Carignano and of Petrus Vesconte, both of Genoa, have thirty-two lines; and these unquestionably were prior to 1331.

[2] These are the colours used in the Perrinus Vesconte Chart (Florence) 1327, in the Catalan Atlas (Paris) 1375, and in practically every one of the hundreds of charts of the period down to 1600 which have survived.

[3] The principal loxodromic centres in some of the best known charts are as follows:—

Pisan Chart (end of thirteenth century), two centres, one in the Aegean, the other near Sardinia; Petrus Veschonte (1311), in the Levant, east of Cyprus; Perrinus Vesconte (1327), near Carcasonne; Mappamundi of the Medicean Atlas (1351), at isthmus of Suez; Giovanni da Carignano (early fourteenth), to the south of Marseilles; Pizigani (1367), near Toulouse; Catalan Atlas (1375, Bibl. Nat., Paris), one near Naples, another to the north of Spain; Pinelli (1384), one in Spain, another south of Naples; Guillelmo Soleri (1385, Archivio di Stato, Florence), one near Bilbao, the other south of Rome, in the sea; Jachobus de Zeroldis (1446, Soc. Colombaria, Florence), to north of Sicily; Catalan Chart (early fifteenth, Florence), between heel of Italy and Greece; Gratiosus Benincasa (1467), off Cape Finisterre; Petrus Roselli (1466, Bibl. Corsini, Florence), to east of Sardinia; Giacomo Bertran (1482), between Sardinia and Sicily; Chart of Badia di Cava (circa 1492), south of Rome, in the sea; Baldasare di Majolo Visconte (1583, Bibl. Naz., Florence), between Palermo and Gaeta; Diego Homen (1558), in Sardinia; the same author (1570) in central Italy.

Islands are often strongly coloured to distinguish them the more readily. The coast lines are depicted with a precision never attempted in the earlier maps, and are most frequently drawn in a peculiar manner by joining together little arcs of circles of different sizes, concave toward the sea, like a series of little bays. Most of these charts, though not all, have the North at the top. Even for a century after the invention of printing all the sailing-charts were drawn by hand; the only exception appears to be in certain charts of Grazioso Benincasa, who seems to have worked by hand upon a printed or etched outline. The chartographers appear to have jealously guarded their individuality. The chartographer's signature is usually given at the left, that is at the West, in some such form as this: *Guillmo Solerij ciujs Maioricaru me fecit Año Añt. Dnj. Mccclxxxv*; or this: *Jachobus Vesconte de Maiollo composuit hanc cartam in Janua anno domini MDLXV.* The inscriptions are mostly written in a Gothic hand of the type current in the fourteenth century. No such charts appeared before the latter end of the thirteenth century, and from that epoch to the end of the sixteenth century they preserved almost unaltered the same features, though the draughtsmanship of the coast lines shows great improvement, and the decorative features received remarkable development. They were highly prized by navigators, as is shown by the circumstance that on the chart of Gabriel de Vallsecha, of 1439, preserved at Palma (Majorca), formerly in the possession of Vespucci, he wrote on it with his own hand: 'For this large geographical skin Amerigo Vespucci has paid 130 gold ducats.' The use of such loxodromic charts is recorded at various dates. Thus the chronicler Nargis, who sailed in the Crusade of St. Louis against Tunis in 1270, tells how the king, being anxious after a storm to know where they were, was shown by the captain the position of the ship on a chart. Vasco da Gama mentions, with some surprise, that the pilot whom he engaged at Malinda to take him to India, in 1498, had a map of India 'without compass lines'.

The question has been debated whether in these loxodromic charts the lines were laid down first, and the coast lines then drawn in over them; or whether the map was first drawn, and the loxodromic lines added afterwards. Nordenskjöld maintains that the lines were drawn over the chart; Theobald Fischer that the chart was drawn over the lines. Kretschmer cites the case of the Atlas of Vesconte de Maiollo, of 1548, now in Florence, having fifteen charts, of which one is unfinished, the lines being drawn, but no map. It must not, however, be concluded that for all charts the lines were drawn first.[1]

[1] Blundevile, in his *Exercises* (1594), gives a blank chart, covered with loxo-

The writer after examining many of the original charts in the museums of London, Paris, Florence, Milan, &c., is convinced that in almost all cases the black lines of the eight principal winds were drawn first, and usually also the eight green lines of the half-winds, but that in many cases the sixteen red lines of the quarter-winds were added after the outlines of the coasts had been drawn on the chart. On comparing together some of the earliest Mediterranean charts one is struck with the extraordinary accuracy of the coastal features which they depict, and the striking similarity which they present one to another, contrasting notably with the crude inaccuracies and variations of all the maps of the antecedent period. It would almost seem as though there had been an accepted standard map of the Mediterranean which successive chartographers had adopted and reproduced. But no such supposition is admissible; for there are differences which exclude the possibility. In the fourteenth century the declination of the needle was unknown; and at that epoch[1] it was relatively small in the middle Mediterranean. The fact of a declination gradually became known; probably being independently observed by pilots and attributed to local error or faulty compasses. But the fact that the declination varied from place to place was quite unknown. That discovery, usually attributed to Columbus,[2] seems to have been more or less known to others. It probably constituted the 'secret' which Sebastian Cabot when dying declared to have been a divine revelation to him. Still less known was the fact that the declination suffered a saecular change; and, unknowingly, the chartographers, working out their maps from observations made at sea, set their coast-lines across the loxodromic lines at angles which differ slightly between one lustrum and another. The differences observable, for example, in the slope of the Adriatic coasts, between the first quarter and the close of the fourteenth century, remain to attest the slow change in the variation of the compass. So long ago as 1624

dromic lines, which he calls 'the shape and figure of the first liniaments of the Mariner's carde, drawn after the old manner', and proceeds to instruct the reader 'how to set down the places of the land or sea therein'.

[1] In the middle-Mediterranean in the thirteenth century the declination was westward. It became zero about the middle of the fourteenth, and was eastward until about the year 1655.

[2] Columbus in his great voyage of 1496 took with him both Genoese and Flemish compasses, and found a discrepancy between them. At a point three degrees west of Flores the Genoese compass showed a westerly deviation, while the Flemish compass showed none. The Flemish pilots probably had adopted the practice, afterwards general in certain ports, and reproved by Dr. Gilbert in 1600, of setting the needle slightly obliquely under the card to compensate for the declination occurring in that region.

THE ROSE OF THE WINDS

Willebrord Snell pointed out that the internal evidence of the charts proves that the compass was used in their construction as early as the thirteenth century; and Signor Enrico Rostagno (of the Biblioteca Laurentiana at Florence) is of opinion that the maps of St. Louis in the Sixth Crusade, 1244-7, were prepared by compass.

Another feature of these sailing-charts is the method of indicating the principal winds by the initials of their names. We have seen how in the early windroses of the prior age the eight, or twelve, or twenty-four winds were named, and how they were represented by heads of cherubs blowing, set around the rose, or framed in the margin of the Mappamundi. This practice was carried on into the fashioning of the sailing-charts, many of which bore brightly coloured margins marked with the names of the winds, or bearing their initials. These initials, or symbols representing them, were usually inscribed in medallions or circles, set in eight of the sixteen subsidiary points of the network, or else placed where the loxodromic lines reached the margin. An example is found in the Majorcan chart of 1385 by Guillelmo Soleri, now at Florence, wherein the *Tramuntana* [*sic*] is named and marked by an eight-point star in red; the East by a red cross, labelled *Levant*; the South is indicated by a face appearing half-way across a circle, marked *Migiorno*; the other points having the names *Grech*, *Axaloch*, *Labetes*, *Ponent*, and *Mestra*, inscribed in Gothic lettering inside coloured circles. Other examples occur in the Majorcan chart of 1447, by Gabriel de Vallsecha, in the Hamy collection; in the chart of Petrus Roselli of 1465 (Fig. 4, Plate II), in the British Museum (Egerton MS., No. 2712); in the Atlas of early American charts in the Egerton MS. (No. 2803) of the British Museum, of about 1508; and in a sixteenth-century map of North Peru, by Bartolomeo Olives of Majorca, now in the Vatican. Where initials are used they are invariably those of the Italian names of the winds; but the *Tramontana* is sometimes marked with a star or a dart, or later with the fleur-de-lis, and the *Levante* almost invariably with a cross. The next change was to place the eight initials, or symbols, around the rosette at the centre of the loxodromic system of lines, as may be seen in the Andrea Bianco chart (Fig. 1, Plate I) of 1436, now in Venice, or in some of the maps in the Venetian Atlas (*circa* 1489) in the British Museum (Egerton MS., No. 73). Another example is afforded by the printed maps of Crete, Patmos, and other islands[1] in the *Isolario* of Bartolommeo da li Sonetti, Venice (?), of 1485. The

[1] The maps in the *Isolario* of Bordone, Venice, 1534, afford another excellent example. On the title-page of that work are two excellent pictures of early Italian compass-roses with the initials of the winds.

third stage was to construct at the centre of the loxodromic net a rose of eight, sixteen, or thirty-two points, drawn as a star with eight rhomboidal rays for the eight principal winds, and with smaller rhombuses or triangles between them for the half-winds and quarter-winds, and to place on the eight principal rays the initials or symbols formerly inscribed in the margins. The decorative treatment given

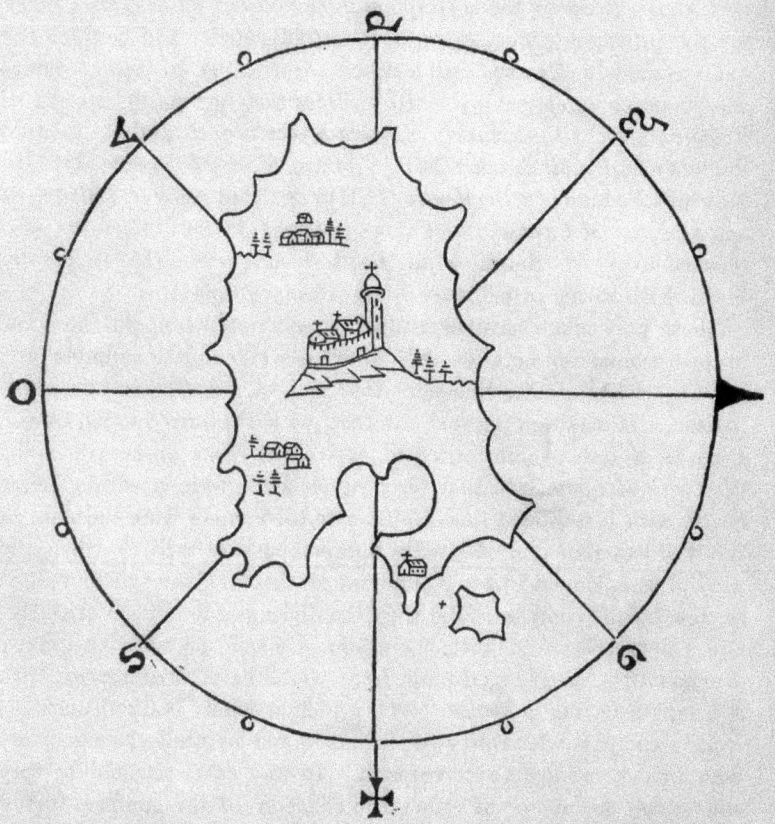

ISLAND OF PATMOS. From the *Isolario* of Bartolommeo da li Sonetti.

to these central windroses has already been noted. With the progress of time the embellishments became more elaborate. The art of the miniaturist lent to them its fascinating aid. We find the centres of the roses, in the later maps, adorned with the device of a ship, or of an armillary sphere, and even with miniatures of the Virgin, or of the Holy Family. Thus ornamented, for example, are the roses of the American chart of 1500 of Juan de la Cosa, reproduced by Lelewel. But, for the most part, except in the charts originating at Mallorca or those with inscriptions in the Catalan dialect, the roses bear on the eight rays of the principal winds the respective initials in Gothic capitals, four of them usually in black, and four in red. The colour treatment of the rhumbs varies, but it is significant to note that in the earlier charts, and indeed commonly, the colours given to the rhumbs of the thirty-two point star correspond with those given to the corresponding loxodromic lines, viz.: black for the principal winds, green for the half-winds, and red for the quarter-winds.[1] Specific instructions for the use of these colours exist in several treatises: Ruscelli's *Espositioni sopra la Geografia di Tolomeo* (1561); Crescentio's *Nautica Mediterranea* (1602); Pantero Pantera's *L'Armata Navale* (1614); Fournier's *Hydrographia* (1671); Fabritius Paduanus's *De Ventis* (1601); Falconi's *Breve Instruzione appartenente al Capitano di Vasselli quadri* (1612). They are also referred to by W. Bourne in his *Regiment of the Sea* (1574), and by Sir H. Manwaring in his *Seaman's Dictionary* (1644).

These particulars have been dwelt upon not merely to show the intimate connexion between the compass-card and the sailing-chart, but to justify certain conclusions that may be drawn from the comparison. It has been pointed out that, with the introduction of the compass into sea-sailing, the old system of eight or twelve winds became inadequate, and that finer subdivisions were needful; hence charts with loxodromic lines to indicate the courses were the natural result of experience in sailing by the compass, as well as being the needful complement in the equipment of the navigator who intended to steer by the compass. Did then the division into sixteen or thirty-two points arise first with the compass itself, or with the map? A map with sixteen loxodromic lines would be of little service with a compass having only the eight principal winds marked upon it; while a compass with thirty-two winds would naturally be associated with a chart marked to correspond. In any case it would be very simple for the maker of either the chart or of the compass to add the extra divisions. Again, why should the chartographers of the beginning of the fourteenth century adopt green lines for the half-winds, and red lines for the quarter-winds, if the compass by which

[1] This convention is, however, not rigidly adhered to, even in the early examples, as we shall see, when considering the various types of roses. For example, in the celebrated Atlas of John Rotz (1542) in the Additional MSS. of the British Museum, No. 11548, the four cardinal winds are painted in gold, and the other four of the eight principal points are blue, while the eight triangles of the half-winds are painted green, and the sixteen triangles of the quarter-winds are red.

these observations had been made, and those with which they were destined to be used, did not possess the same colorations on their corresponding rhumbs? The correspondence in the choice of colours is most significant, as it suggests that both compass and chart developed *pari passu*. But that development would not be in the least likely to occur so long as the compass remained a mere floating needle of the primitive Levant type, or even so long as the needle was pivoted to move over a fixed card, or within a box having fixed graduations on its edge, like an astrolabe, as in Peregrinus's compass of 1269. The necessary step in evolution must have been that of the fastening of the movable card with its coloured rose upon the pivoted needle; and that step was subsequent to 1269. If we may infer that step from the appearance on the sailing-charts of the thirty-two loxodromic lines, then the date cannot be later than 1311, the year of Petrus Veschonte's chart, and may be earlier, if the Pisan chart, now in Paris, commonly supposed to date from the end of the twelfth century, is really so old. The tradition, which is strong in fixing the year 1302 for the 'invention' of the mariners' compass by the unknown navigator of Amalfi, seems therefore to be well founded so far as regards two of its principal features: (1) that the 'invention' consisted in the mounting of the *rosa ventorum* upon the needle; (2) that this 'invention' took place at the end of the thirteenth, or at the very beginning of the fourteenth, century. That it was made at Amalfi must remain a matter of tradition: for the matters which have been urged as evidence in support are all fallacious. For instance, it has been urged that geographically the only place where the North East wind blows from Greece, where the South West wind blows from Africa, and the North wind across the mountains (the Apennines), giving rise to the respective names of *Greco, Africo*, and *Tramontana*, must have been Amalfi. On this it suffices to observe that those denominations were in general use as the Italian names of the winds at least one or two centuries earlier. Another allegation, that the civic arms of the city of Amalfi bear emblazoned the figure of a compass, has long ago been shown to be wholly devoid of foundation in fact. But the well-attested tradition embodied in the line, attributed to Panormitan,

Prima dedit nautis usum magnetis Amalphis,

remains undisturbed. It seems to have escaped the notice of recent writers that, according to Crescentio, the addition of the eight half-winds and the sixteen quarter-winds, bringing up the number of points to thirty-two, originated[1] with the Amalphitanians. Certain

---

[1] Op. cit., p. 157. 'Ultimamente in Amalfi hanno collocato tra questi otto

it is that the compass with the pivoted card, marked with the winds in a rose of eight principal points in the Italian manner, and with subdivisions corresponding to half-winds and quarter-winds, originated in Southern Italy at the end of the thirteenth century; and that the characteristic features of the compass-card, including the system of colouring adopted, were developed in connexion with the loxodromic sailing-charts of the Italian navigators.

Origin of the Distinctive Marks used on Compass-Cards.

It has been mentioned above that the majority of the early Italian compass-roses bore, in Gothic capitals, the initials of the Italian names of the eight principal winds. There were variants, however, in the usage. The East point, instead of being inscribed with L for *Levante* was more commonly marked with a cross. The West point, though almost always marked with a P for *Ponente*, was rarely indicated by the symbol of the setting sun. The South West point is usually marked with A for *Africo*, less often with L for *Libeccio*, and very rarely with G for *Garbino*. The South point is usually marked with O for *Ostro*, and but rarely with M for *Mezzodì*. The three invariables are the North East with G for *Greco*, the South East with S for *Scirocco*, and the North West with M for *Maestro*. The most variable of all in the manner of its indication is the North point. We are so accustomed to see the North point marked on the compass-card with a fleur-de-lis that it is somewhat surprising to be told that the compass-card existed two hundred years without any fleur-de-lis, that symbol being, in fact, a late addition. In the pre-compass era the names for the North, as inscribed on maps were either astronomical, such as *Septentrio* (from the seven stars) or *Arctos* (the Bear), or were the names of winds such as *Boreas*, *Hyperboreus*, *Aparctias*, *Aquilo*, or *Tramontana*. The name *Tramontana* became applied not only to the wind that blew across the mountains, and hence to the geographical North, but also to the North Pole Star (Stella Tramontana), and, by metonymy, even to the magnetic needle itself, because it pointed northwards. None of these various names for the North lent its initials to mark the North point except *Tramontana*. In windroses, and in early compass-roses, the initial T is often used to denote the North point, but never are the initials

venti principali altri otto, detti da loro meziventi.' On p. 255 he adds :—' Può essere poi che in Amalfi, per più commodità de' Naviganti, fusse l' una [la carta] e l' altra [la bussola] in 32 punti o venti scompartita.'

of the other names *Boreas, Septentrio*, &c. so used. Other symbols, however, are found quite as frequently as the letter T, and sometimes in association with it. A star, or a group of seven stars, is sometimes found. A star, for instance, marks the North in the Planisphere of the *Cosmographie d'Azaph* (MS. Paris, twelfth century), and in the Mappamundi of Marino Sanudo, 1321 (MS. Brussels). A group of seven stars appears in the compass-card (Fig. 11, Plate VI) printed in the chapter ' Dei Venti e della Bussola da navicare' by Giovanni Quintino à Sofo in the *Della Guerra di Rhodi* of Jacopo Fontano (Venice, 1545). A star or a group of seven stars appears in the compass-cards of the Catalan type mentioned below. A more frequent mark for the North may be described as a triangle representing an arrow-head or a dart. This mark is not found in the pre-magnetic windroses, and may therefore be regarded as distinctively denoting a magnetic needle. A narrow, dart-like triangle, extending from the middle of the rose to the North, is found in the sailing-chart (late fifteenth century) in the Archives of Lucerne (Figs. 4 & 5, Plate III), and in the similar chart at Upsala; also in Fontano's book just mentioned. Another occurs in the chart of Juan de la Cosa (1500) (Fig. 7, Plate IV). A broad triangle, like an arrow-head, marks the North in the compass-roses of the Catalan or Majorcan type. A commoner form is that in which the North triangle or rhumb of the rose is painted black, as in the rose of the Pinelli chart of 1384 (Fig. 2, Plate II), the still earlier rose of Nicolao di Combitis in the Marciana library at Venice, the compass on the chart of Jachobus de Giraldis, of 1426,[1] in the same library, and on that of Battista Agnese, of 1545, also in Venice; also in the rose of the Agnese chart now in Stockholm. A triangle for the North is one of the four symbols found in the MS. Atlas—the oldest atlas of the New World—in the British Museum.[2]

Occasionally the triangular or arrow-head mark is associated with the star-symbol,[3] as in the rose of the Catalan Atlas (1375), and in

---

[1] In this instance the coloured rose appears to be of later date than the chart itself.
[2] Egerton MSS., No. 2803, dated 1508.
[3] The close association of the symbols of the star and of the dart with the North is attested by a remarkable etching in a book on Painting, by Marco Boschini (Venice, 1660), called *La Carta del navegar pitoresco*, p. 616, representing a female figure, emblematic of the North wind, with a javelin; while above is an eight-point star. Opposite it is the following quatrain:—

Voi che 'l me rapresenta, in bela forma,
La Tramontana, che stabile, e immota
Sia scorta al Marinier, al bon Peota,
Come stela, che in mar xè vera norma.

that of the chart of Petrus Roselli (Fig. 4, Plate II) in the British Museum, also in that of Giorgio Callapoda (1552) (Fig. 10, Plate V) in the Museo Civico at Venice. Also, occasionally, the triangle is associated with the initial T, as in the rose of Andrea Bianco (1436), in that of Giacomo Castaldi (1564), and in the chart engraved on copper by Nicolaus di Nicolay (1560) at Venice. The use of a black triangle for the North is recognized also by various writers. In the *De Ventis* of Fabritius Paduanus (Bononiae, 1601) occur[1] the phrases: 'Nigredo illa Tramontanam denotat', 'Nigredo illa Septentrionem', 'per nigrum radium intelligendo Tramontanam'. A trident occasionally appears instead of a dart, to mark the North, as in the rose on the sailing-chart of the Monastery of Badia di Cava Tirrena (*circa* 1492) (Fig. 3, Plate II), and in the rose of the late fifteenth-century chart, now in Paris, said to have been in the possession of Richelieu; also in the Atlas of Joannes de Oliva, 1613, in the British Museum (Egerton MS., No. 819). Yet one other symbol for the North is found, occasionally, in the use of a human head, as in the strange compass-card (Fig. 12, Plate VI) of Pierre Garcie, the pilot of Rouen, 1584. A head also appears, surmounted by a dart, in the interior of the compass printed in the *De Ventis et Navigatione*, of Michael Angelus Blondus, at Venice, 1546. That mariners regarded the North as the head is emphasized by the fact that in a compass-rose of João de Lisboa, in his *Tratado da Agulha de marear* (1514), the North point, marked with a fleur-de-lis, is inscribed *cabeça* (head), the South point *pee* (foot), while the East and West are respectively inscribed *braço de leste* and *braço daloeste* [sic].

In all modern compasses, practically without exception, the device used to indicate the North is the fleur-de-lis, or as the sailors often call it, the Prince of Wales's feathers. No one has hitherto been able to account for the introduction of this symbol; it is not known to exist[2] on any compass or chart before the sixteenth century, the supposed earliest one being that on the chart in the Bibliothèque Nationale in Paris, which is believed to have belonged to Cardinal Richelieu, conjectured to be of date 1493; but its form suggests a trident rather than a lily. Many fallacious inferences having been drawn from the occurrence of the fleur-de-lis, it is important to

---

[1] Similarly, in the *Isolario* of Benedetto Bordone (Venetia, 1534),

'laltra che è tutta negra è tramontana'.

[2] Father Bertelli says (*Studi storici*, 1894, p. 204) that the earliest known to him is on a Majorcan chart in the Library of Parma (No. 1620), of late fifteenth century; but this does not seem to have been reproduced in any of the published collections of charts.

scrutinize closely the circumstances. The fleur-de-lis has been for centuries a heraldic emblem. It was in use for regal decorations in the East before the time of the Crusades. Adalbert de Beaumont[1] has traced back its use as a decorative emblem to Byzantine times, and has derived it from the lotos ornament of Egypt. In particular it was adopted by the kings of France, by the dukes of Anjou, and by the Bourbon family. It seems to have been appropriated by Philippe Auguste, at whose coronation, at Rheims in 1179, the practice began of strewing with golden fleurs-de-lis on a field of azure all the banners, hangings, and scutcheons used in that ceremony. But earlier than this, Carolus Magnus had given the fleur-de-lis to the city of Florence,[2] not so much as being a lily but rather as emblematic of royalty, with the motto *Florida florenti floreat Florentia flore*. From Louis VII to Henry IV the emblem preserved its primitive form in the royal blazonry of France. Louis IX ordained that the fleur-de-lis should be borne by all the princes of royal blood. Whence then comes the appearance of the fleur-de-lis as the chief device on the modern compass-card? The answer which may hesitatingly be given, after examination of the various treatments of the marking of the North point, is that it is a purely decorative development[3] of the dart, the star, and the T of earlier use. The T of *Tramontana*, with its drooping appendages, or serifs, lent itself to this development, which may be traced through various incomplete stages. Only after the year 1500 does the fully-formed fleur-de-lis appear, and then most frequently in the Portuguese compass-roses. Doubtless when the usage of a fleur-de-lis had once found acceptance, political influences would tend to promote its employment.

[1] *Recherches sur l'origine du blason, et en particulier sur la fleur de lis*, Paris, 1853. On p. 105, quoting a dissertation by Bullet, of 1791, de Beaumont states that the original form was *fleur de li*, or *fleur de roi*; the word *li* in Celtic signifying king. Ducange, in his *Dissertation sur Saint Louis*, confirms this by saying that after the first Crusade, when Christian heraldry began, the heralds adopted as a symbol of sovereignty the emblem which had struck them as having this significance.

[2] It may be remarked that on several of the decorative charts of the fifteenth century—for example, Dulcert's, of 1339, and the still earlier map of Giovanni da Carignano, of Genoa—on which the loxodromic rosettes bear no roses, and in others of the fifteenth century which bear compass-roses devoid of fleurs-de-lis, the fleur-de-lis is found marked on the banners that indicate the political standing of some of the cities. The banner of Paris bears *azure* five fleurs-de-lis *or*, and that of Florence bears *argent* a single lily *gules* of the peculiar Florentine form with two projecting stamens.

[3] Another strange development of the ornament at the North point is the bunch of grapes, which appears on the rose in the chart of Ruiz de Estrada e Peñato, of 1525, reproduced in Nordenskjöld's *Periplus*.

It must be borne in mind, however, that there is a distinction to be drawn between the designs of the roses actually used on the 'flie', as Tudor writers called it, of an actual compass and the designs drawn in the roses of the sailing-charts. The former must of necessity present a circular periphery in order to turn freely within the compass box, while in the case of the latter there is nothing to hinder the draughtsman from depicting salient ornaments that project forth beyond the circumference of the rose. On the rose of the Andrea Bianco chart in Venice (1436), the letters T and L are tacked on to the apices of the North and East points respectively. Similarly on a rose of a sailing-chart of Africa, of 1527, at Weimar, a lily and a cross stand out as excrescences outside the circle; while in another chart (sixteenth century) in the Biblioteca Marciana a triangle extends at the North, a Latin cross at the East, and a large P at the West. The celebrated Atlas of John Rotz (1542), in the British Museum, illustrates 'the manner for to knowe the Wyndes of all the points of the Sey compass' with a gorgeously-coloured rose having a golden lily and a golden cross standing outside the periphery. Projecting spear-heads, pyramids, crosses, and lilies, such as abound on the roses of the florid charts of the sixteenth century would be impossible on a real compass-card. So, though the roses of the charts may be in the main pictures of the compass-cards of the day, they must be received with caution. So far as the author is aware there is not preserved in any museum in the world any actual compass or compass-card older than the late sixteenth century. The rude compass (Fig. 12, Plate VI) of Pierre Garcie of Rouen in his treatise *Le Grand Routier, pilotage et encrage de la Mer,* of 1584, is doubtless printed from the very wood-block which was used to print the compass-cards in that port. It is possibly the oldest compass-card in existence. Internal evidence shows that in many cases the sea-charts were revised or improved by later hands, as further discoveries extended the knowledge of the coast-lines; and in many cases the decorative embellishments are of subsequent date, as appears to be the case with the fine compass-rose on the early fifteenth-century chart of Jachobus de Giraldis. The gorgeous fleur-de-lis on the map painted on vellum by the order of Henri II, reproduced in Jomard's *Monuments de la Géographie,* bespeaks the courtier in the artist; while the splendid blue lily depicted in 1529 by Diego Ribera in his map—the famous map on which Pope Julius II drew the line to decide the dispute between Spain and Portugal, as to their respective title to discovered lands—equally proclaims that it is really no inherent part of the compass-rose which it adorns.

As to the arguments which have been founded on the circumstance that a fleur-de-lis is so generally found on compass-cards, one may now see of what value they are. Father Fournier, in his *Hydrographie* (1671), p. 399, argues thus:

Puis que toutefois les arguments qui se tirent des monuments, comme pierres, marbres, sepulchres, traditions immemoriales, et choses semblables, ont plus de force que ceux que nous pourrions auoir de quelque auteur passionné pour son pays: Je dis que la Fleur de lis, de la pointe de l'aiguille dont toutes les Nations de l'Europe se seruent pour monstrer le Nord, témoigne assez que ce sont les François qui l'ont bastie de la sorte, et que c'est d'eux qu'ils ont appris l'vsage : car à quel propos les Matelots de Noruegue, Danemarc, Angleterre, Italie: bref tous les Europeans auroient-ils mis en ce lieu plustost les armes de France que de leur Nation. Outre qu'il est constant que les mots de Nord, Sud, Est, et Oüest, dont on se sert sur l'Océan pour monstrer les Runs des vents sont mots Français, desquels on se servoit du temps de Charlemagne.

Venanson, in his work *De l'invention de la boussole nautique*, Naples, 1808, argues that in 1302, the traditional date when the compass was 'invented' by the mythical Flavio di Gioia, the kingdom of Naples, in which Amalfi is situated, was governed by French princes of the house of Anjou, and hence the reason why the fleur-de-lis is marked on the card! This erroneous view appears to have originated with Gassendi.

How little the fleur-de-lis was considered as pertaining to the compass may be judged from the remarkable group of etchings published about the year 1600 under the title of *Nova Reperta*, etched by P. Galle from the drawings of Joannes Stradanus, and dedicated to Aloysio Alamanno, Florentino. They relate to the recent discoveries of America, Lapis Polaris (the Lodestone), Gunpowder, the Printing Press, Clocks, Guaiacum, Distillation, Silkgrowing, and Harness, 'prisco operta cuncta saeculo'. In these etchings appear three figures of the mariners' compass. None have fleur-de-lis. The compass on the title-page is a simple eight-point star with an arrow-head at the North point and three stars at the South.

The cross at the East point underwent many variations of form. It appears usually as a Greek or a Maltese cross, sometimes as a Latin cross, often as a cross pattee, rarely as a cross fitchee. In the rose of Cecco d'Ascoli (*see* p. 11) it resembles a cross-handled dagger. Occasionally it takes the form of a St. Andrew's cross attached outside the periphery of the rose, as in the Weimar map of Africa. It sometimes degenerated into an arrangement of intersecting circles, or into a pair of parallel cross-lines. In a compass preserved in the Galilei Museum in Florence, of date supposed to be about 1650, it appears as a pair of dolphins. It continued to be marked, even on English compasses, down to the eighteenth century. In a fine card in the author's collection, engraved by John Sellers about 1660, the cross has degenerated into a couple of S-shaped marks above and below the East point, a form which survived even to the nineteenth century. Another English card in the author's collection, of date about 1640, has the usual thirty-two English names in initials surrounding a thirty-two point rose, the four cardinal rays of which are marked with the Latin initials S(eptentrio), O(riens), M(eridies), and O(ccidens); while the North point bears a fleur-de-lis, the East a cross, the South an arrow-head, and the West a heart-shaped ornament.

As distinctive marks for the West point one occasionally meets with a P, or a double P (from which possibly the heart-shaped ornament is derived), or sometimes the figure of the setting sun with rays, or sometimes a plain circle. Cleirac in his *Us et Coustumes de la Mer* (1661) states that the West point is marked with an imperial double-headed eagle.

Riccioli in his *Almagestum* (1651), and Gallucci, *Della Fabrica et Uso di diversi Stromenti di Astronomia* (1598), speak of compasses which possess, erected over the centre of the needle, an upright stylus to carry a little flag to indicate the direction of the wind. A picture of a compass so designed is given in Pigafetta's *Premier voyage autour du monde*, 1519–22, on p. 286 of the Paris edition of 1801.

Of singularities in the design of compass-cards a quaint instance is afforded by the woodcut print of Pierre Garcie (Fig. 12, Plate VI) already mentioned. It bears in the centre a crude human figure with the head to the North, and arms spread out from the elbows to the East and West. The East and West names appear to have been reversed in printing. Another strange compass-rose is that printed in the *De Ventis et Navigatione* of Blondus (Venice, 1546). It has twenty-six points marked with the Latin names of twenty-six winds, and is described as 'Pixis vel Buxolus, instrumentum et dux navigantium'. This he regards as a new compass, and speaks of those who formerly sailed 'cum observatione antiqui pyxidis et cultu Ursae minoris'. He alleges reasons for abandoning the old compass with eight or twelve winds, and for preferring this new pyxis with its twenty-six winds. In the middle is an inner circle in which are inscribed the usual eight symbols of the Italian rose, the T of the *Tramontana* being replaced by a javelin-head; and in the centre of this there is drawn a human face with the top of the head towards the North.

Having now reviewed the development of the compass-card and its details, we may attempt some classification of the forms which appear prior to 1600. Amid the vast variety of treatment we may admit three leading types:

1. *Italian type with eight winds.* In this type a star of eight rays is represented. It is the basis of many more developed forms. The Lucerne chart of late fifteenth century gives an example (Fig. 5, Plate III), the North ray being black, the other seven of gold, and without initials. The rose of Cecco d'Ascoli of 1521 (page 11) is another example. The eight-point rose of Andrea Benincasa, of Ancona, 1476, which has four rays blue and four red, with internal appendages of an arrow, a cross, and a circle for the setting sun, is another. An eight-point rose in the chart of date 1501–2, in the collection of M. Hamy, has a dart added externally at the North. The rose of Nicolaus de Nicolay, 1560, has eight half-winds in addition.

2. *Italian type with thirty-two winds.* The characteristic feature here is the arrangement of three series of coloured triangles, marked with the initials or symbols of the eight principal winds. Typical examples are the Andrea Bianco rose of 1436, with eight winds in gold, eight in green, sixteen in red; the rose of the anonymous chart, of the second half of the fifteenth century, in the Biblioteca Ambrosiana (No. F. 260, infra No. 2), with the same colouring, save that the North rhumb is black; and the rose of the chart of Badia di Cava Tirrena (Fig. 3, Plate II), of the same epoch, with eight black, eight green, and sixteen red. To the same type, but with some modifications, belong the roses of Matheus Prunes, 1561, in the possession of Prince Corsini; and the undated rose in the Museo Civico of Venice, reproduced by Kretschmer (Plate XXX of his collection). A design by Cabot (see Jomard, xx. 1), of early sixteenth century, adopts the three ranges of triangles, but uses a different colouring. A fine sixteenth-century rose in the Spanish MSS. of the Bibliothèque de l'Arsenal at Paris (No. 8813) has eight winds blue, eight gold, and sixteen red. The Atlas of John Rotz (1542) has a rose with four of the principal winds gold, the other four blue, the eight half-winds green, and the sixteen quarter-winds red, but with the late addition of a lily in gold. João de Lisboa's rose, of 1514, with four black, four gold, eight green, and sixteen red, decorated with a lily, affords a Portuguese example of this type.

3. *Catalan or Majorcan type.* This is characterized by having the four cardinal winds in blue and the other four winds in red or gold, without any triangles for the half-winds or quarter-winds, and having a broad arrow-head at the North. This type bears no initials. Typical specimens are that (Fig. 4, Plate II) on the chart of Petrus Roselli, of 1465, in the British Museum (Egerton MS., No. 2712), and the

almost identical one, of 1466, by the same hand, in the possession of Prince Corsini. Above the arrow-head for the North, in these examples, is a cluster of seven stars. Closely akin are the roses of the Catalan Atlas in Paris—one of them the oldest known compass-rose—and the rose of the Berlin sea-chart (*circa* 1450), described and figured by Kretschmer. Both these have crosses at the East. The Catalan chart of 1429 (Florence, Bibl. Naz., No. 16); the Minorcan chart of Giacomo Bertran, of 1482 (Florence, Archivio di Stato, No. 7); the chart of M. di Majorca, of 1487 (ibid., No. 8); the chart of Angelus Eufredutius, of 1556, at Mantua; that of Vincenzo de Demetrio Volzio di Ragusa, 1607 (Florence, Archivio di Stato, No. 19), are all close to the type. So are the roses of two fifteenth-century manuscripts in Paris—that in the Arsenale (Italian MSS., No. 42), cited by Bertelli, and that in the Gregorio Dati manuscript of 1420 in the Bibliothèque Nationale. A modification of this type, in which the subsidiary winds are added, is exemplified in a form used by Juan de la Cosa (1500), having the eight principal winds in blue and gold, the eight half-winds in red, and the quarter-winds in white.

4. *Black dart type.* Although in some of the roses of the other types a black triangle indicates the North, those of this type are characterized by the presence of a large, narrow, black triangle extending from the centre of the rose to the North point; the other winds being represented by fifteen, or sometimes thirty-one, smaller triangles, usually of equal size, ranged round the periphery. This type occurs chiefly between 1500 and 1600. A typical example is presented by the roses (Fig. 8, Plate IV) of the exquisite little anonymous atlas, of date about 1540, in the British Museum (Egerton MS., No. 2854). Another is the 'bossolo da nauigar moderno' depicted in Bordone's *Isolario* (Venice, 1534). Other examples are found in the roses (Figs. 5 & 6, Plate III) of the Lucerne chart (late sixteenth century); the chart at Upsala; the chart of Agnese Battista at Stockholm; the 'Richard King' chart of 1501-2, in the collection of M. Hamy; the charts of Giacomo Castaldi, of 1561 and 1564; the chart of G. Sideri, of 1562 (Egerton MS., No. 2856); the chart of Jachobus Vesconte de Maiollo, made in Rome in 1562 (Additional MSS., No. 1916); the map of Diego Homen (Egerton MS., No. 2858); also in the sketch of a compass in the Italian manuscript, fol. 43, of uncertain date, at the end of Egerton MS., No. 73. It is of some interest to note that while this type occurs along with the arrow-head (Catalan) type in the charts of Juan de la Cosa, in 1500 and 1520, it reappears surmounted by a fine fleur-de-lis in his chart of 1529.

5. *Messina type.* In the middle are the eight symbols of the Italian winds: dart, cross, O, and P, in black; and G, S, A, and M, in red. Around the outside are sixteen small triangles, sometimes all in white, sometimes in alternating blue and gold, with sixteen smaller rhumbs, usually in red, between them, for the quarter-winds. To this class belong the roses (Fig. 8, Plate V) in the charts of Joannes Martines, of 1567 and of 1578, the latter being Harleian MS., No. 3489; and those of Giacomo Russo, of Messina, 1557, in the collection of M. Hamy.

6. *Portuguese type.* This form, of subsequent date to the preceding, and which occurs also in English compass-cards, is practically the Catalan type, but with a fleur-de-lis replacing the arrow-head. A typical example is the rose of Demetrius Voltius, of 1593, reproduced in Nordenskjöld's *Periplus*. Another is that in the anonymous sixteenth-century chart in Florence (Archivio di Stato, No. 17). An old compass, probably English, of early seventeenth century, in the Galilei Museum in Florence, is of the same type, having four winds (including the lily) in blue and four in red. In the *Arte pratica de navegar* of Luis Sarrão Pimentel (Lisboa, 1681) an almost identical rose is engraved. An actual compass-card by John Sellers (*circa* 1660), in the writer's collection, is also closely akin, but is devoid of colour. It is singular to find in the *De Magnete* of Dr. William Gilbert, of 1600, p. 185, a card of the same pattern used in a dipping-needle.

Besides these types many others appear, of intermediate forms, or with mixed characteristics. Thus in a Portuguese atlas in the Bibliothèque de l'Arsenal, at Paris (*circa* 1520), we find a rose with a black dart, but with other features like those of the Italian roses of thirty-two winds. The roses of the charts preserved in the various museums of Venice present great variety, both in colouring and detail of form, some showing Arabic or Moorish influence. It is not possible to assign definitely any special typical design to any particular port, whether Naples, Genoa, Marseilles, or any other. Nor, though in many cases the identity of the artist is unmistakable, did the designers of these roses always adhere to one type. Indeed, some of them seem to have gloried in inventing new designs from page to page of their atlases. After 1600 nearly every compass bore a fleur-de-lis, and before the seventeenth century was over all coloration and all use of the Italian initials disappeared. Since 1650 the compass-cards of all European nations have presented little variation of any kind.

It is to be hoped that further research will be made as to the existence of actual compass-cards of early times. A compass, presumably English, with a coloured card, exists in the Galilei Museum in Florence; others are said to exist in Munich and in Madrid. Probably others remain unknown in museums or private collections. Possibly in Havre, Rouen, Bruges, Hamburg, Lisbon, Marseilles, Genoa, Naples, Venice or other old maritime centre, there may be found sailing-compasses with roses coloured in the ancient manner. The study of any such will further elucidate the problems of the origin and development here considered.

Note, added February 1914.

At the date when this paper was written the author had not seen the privately-printed work *Der Compass,* issued in 1911 by Herr A. Schück of Hamburg, which consists of a series of forty-six magnificent plates in colours, illustrating with a wealth of detail the construction of the compass and the design of the compass-card from the earliest time to the present date, together with a Catalogue describing the hundreds of figures in those plates. Nothing in this remarkable and elaborate repertory runs counter to the main conclusions expressed in the author's paper. But Herr Schück puts forth a new and ingenious conjecture as to the origin of the *fleur-de-lis* mark, the introduction of which on the compass-rose at the end of the fifteenth century is discussed in the author's paper. Herr Schück suggests that this mark is essentially a representation of the form of the primitive floating compass, and that it depicts a lancet-shaped magnetic needle supported between its two wooden floats. While the author does not admit that this hypothesis has been proven by Herr Schück, he agrees that Herr Schück at least has made out a case worthy of consideration. Amongst the compass-roses described by Herr Schück is one in an early sixteenth-century Portuguese atlas in the Riccardi Library in Florence, bearing at its North point the device here copied. The dart is in black; the two side-appendages are gold-coloured. Numerous similar forms, which are strictly not *fleurs-de-lis* in their intention, could be cited from other early examples. If this should hereafter be proved to have been a customary form of the *rainette,* or *calamita,* which preceded the pivoted compass, in the Mediterranean, his contention will be much more than a plausible suggestion.

S. P. T.

Plate I

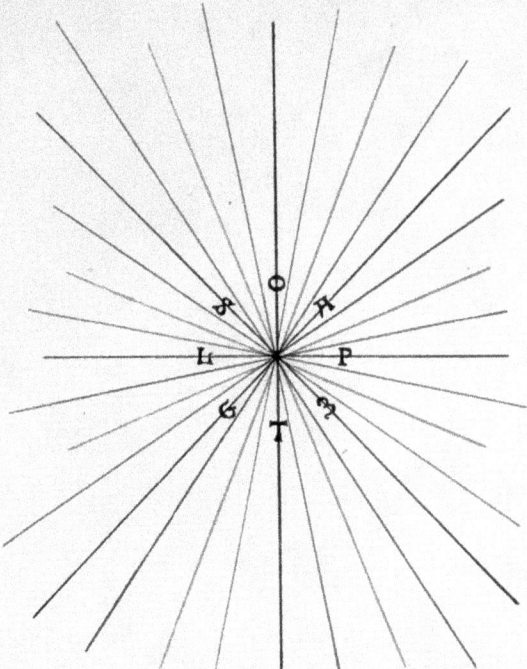

Fig. 1
Loxodromic rosette with initials of Italian names of the winds, from sailing-chart of Andrea Bianco, of 1436.

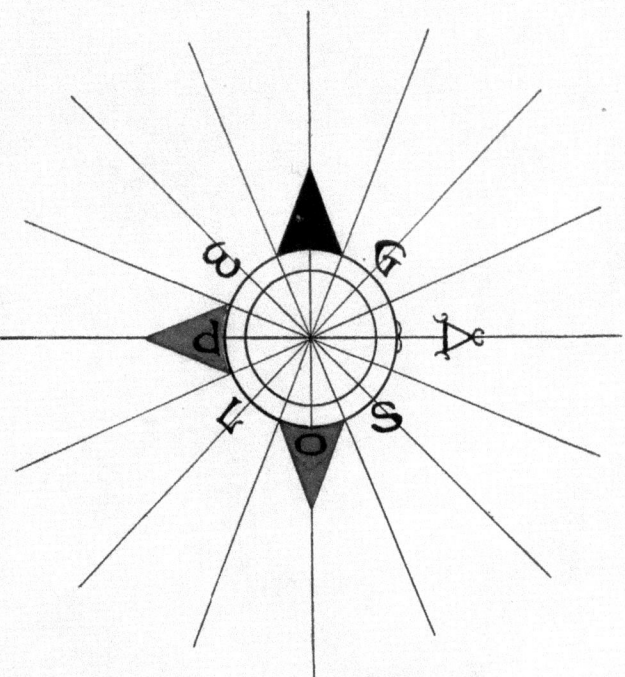

Fig. 2
Windrose from the anonymous sailing-chart of 1384, known as the Portolano Pinelli, now in Paris.

Plate II

Fig. 3

Rose from the sailing-chart (circa 1492) in the Archivio della Badia di Cava Tirrena. (Italian thirty-two point type.)

Fig. 4

Rose from the sailing-chart of Petrus Roselli, of 1465. Egerton MS. No. 2712 in the British Museum. (Catalan or Majorcan type.)

Plate III

Fig. 5
Rose from sailing-chart in the archives of Lucerne, circa 1500.
(Eight-point type, with black dart.)

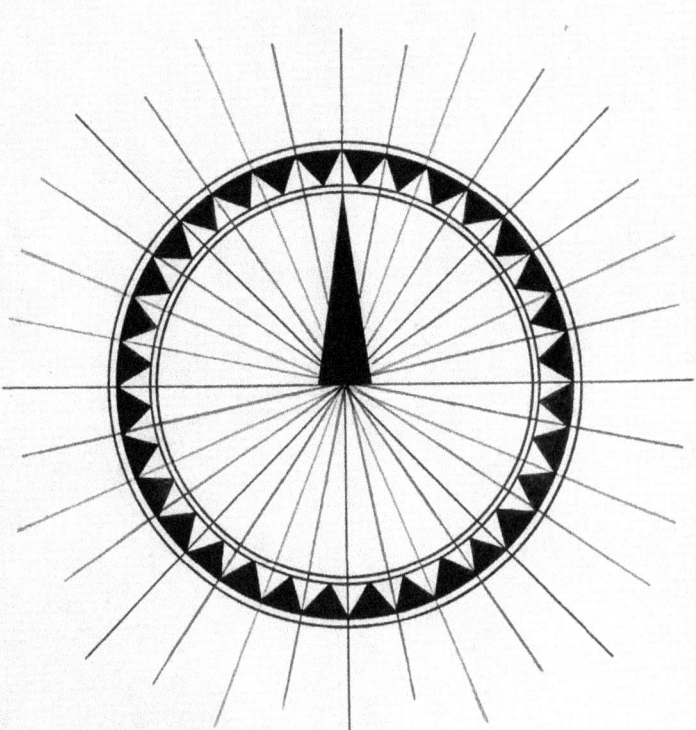

Fig. 6
Rose from sailing-chart in the archives of Lucerne, circa 1500.
(Black-dart type.)

Plate IV

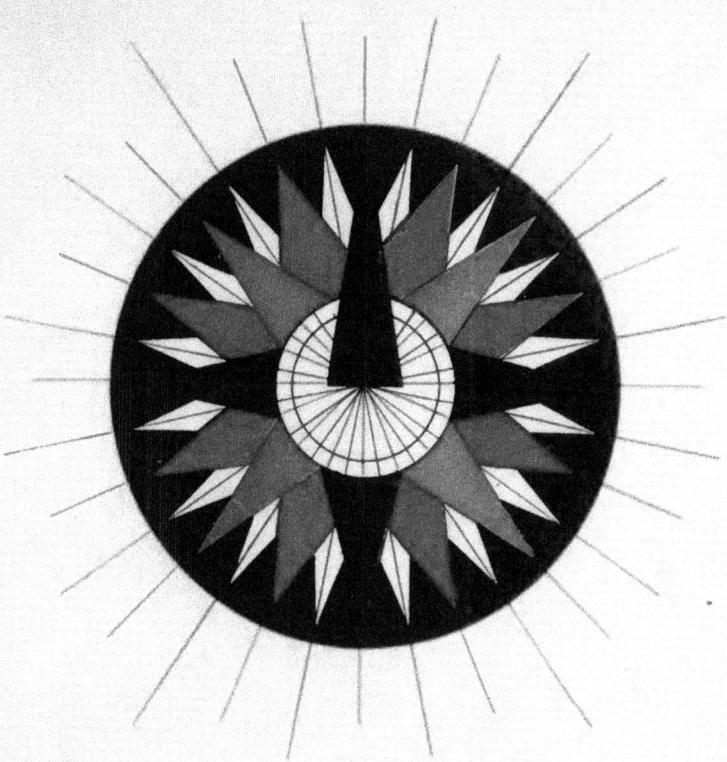

Fig. 7
Rose from sailing-chart of Juan de la Cosa, of 1500.

Fig. 8
Rose from sailing-chart, 1540. Egerton MS. No. 2854.
in the British Museum. (Black-dart type.)

Plate V

Fig. 9
Rose from sailing-chart of Joannes Martines, 1567.
(Messina type.)

Fig. 10
Rose from sailing-chart of Giorgio Calapoda, 1552.

Plate VI

Fig. 11

Figura della Bussola, from the *Dei venti e della bussola da navicare* of Giovanni Quintino. Venice, 1545.

Fig. 12

Compass-card printed on title-page of *Le Grand Routier, Pilotage et Encrage de la Mer*, of Pierre Garcie. Rouen, 1584.

www.ingramcontent.com/pod-product-compliance
Lightning Source LLC
Chambersburg PA
CBHW081024040426
42444CB00014B/3345